THE PEACE KIT

by John Lampen

Second edition, 2005

Quaker Books

First published 1992
by Quaker Home Service
Revised edition published 2005 by Quaker Books
Friends House, 173 Euston Road, London NW1 2BJ
www.quaker.org.uk

© John Lampen 1992, 2005
Illustrations © Cormac Downey 1992

ISBN: 0 85245 372 8

The moral rights of the author are asserted in accordance with the Copyright, Designs and Patents Act 1988. All rights reserved. No part of this book may be reproduced or utilised, in any form or by any means, electronic or mechanical, without permission in writing from the publisher. Reviewers may quote brief passages. Enquiries should be addressed to the Publications Manager, Quaker Books, Friends House, 173 Euston Road, London NW1 2BJ

Contents

Feelings
 page 5

Caring and Listening
 page 13

Building Bridges
 page 21

Meeting Fear and Prejudice
 page 33

Putting Things Right
 page 43

Becoming a More Peaceful Person
 page 52

For your own ideas
 page 62

Acknowledgements, and Discovering More
 page 63

Index of problems discussed
 page 64

The Peace Kit

Chapter One:
FEELINGS

I'd like to start by telling you a story. When my daughter Clare was eight, years ago, she came home from school very indignant about her head teacher. We asked what he had done. "Well, somebody got Julie's new sweater during playtime and took a pair of scissors and cut it into bits. And Mr Robinson found out it was Peter, and he shouted at him in front of the whole school and took him into his room and gave him the cane." What had made her so angry? "Nobody is that naughty unless they're very upset about something. Peter doesn't normally do things like that. Mr Robinson should have found out what was upsetting Peter and helped him instead of beating him." (In those days head teacher were allowed to punish children by hitting them with a cane; in some schools it was done quite often to boys).

I wonder if you would have thought the same as Clare? We lived and worked in a place for teenagers who had got into trouble with the police or had other serious problems. So Clare had often heard us discussing how to understand and help them. And unlike you she knew Peter. He was a quiet little boy who didn't make friends easily, but he didn't try to hurt or annoy other people. And she knew something else, which Mr Robinson should have known too. This was that Peter's family had been looking forward to a new baby; she had been born a week before but she died after three days, and Peter's mother was still very ill.

This book is about things to do to make the world about you more peaceful. You can get instruction books for many things nowadays from making patchwork quilts to mending the car. If you look at a book about (say) using a computer, you will probably find that the first chapter gives you some idea of how a computer works. This may be the hardest part of the book to understand, but it makes things easier when you read the rest. So I want to look first at how unpeaceful feelings work, to help us understand how to deal with them.

Let's use the story of Julie, Peter and the sweater to do this. It's a sad story, but it makes us ask questions: why did Peter cut up the sweater? Could someone have stopped this from happening? How did Peter feel afterwards? What could be done for Julie? Why did Mr Robinson beat Peter? What good did he think it would do? What else could he have done? Is it certain that Peter won't do something like this again?

Feeling bad and doing wrong

"Feeling bad" can mean different things, either feeling unhappy and hurt, or feeling that you would like to do something wrong. But sometimes they are almost the same thing. What do you feel like when someone calls you a bad name, or gives you a big disappointment? (You might like to think about this for a moment before you read on.) I've asked a lot of young people that question. There are a lot of different answers: "miserable", "angry", "nearly crying", "it didn't bother me", "I'd like to hit them" and so on. But most of the answers are one of two kinds: either you hold the bad feeling inside you and it is like a painful lump in your middle; or you try to hit back by saying or doing something to hurt someone else.

I'm sure you have seen this at school. If a boy or girl says something mean to two of your friends, one of them may become very quiet and drop out of the group. And the other may go red and shout something back to hurt the person who started it. That may not be a very peaceful reaction, but at least it's fair! But suppose the first person is much bigger than you? Suppose it's a teacher who upsets you? Then it might be risky to say something back. So just possibly you might go off and be unkind to another child instead, perhaps your brother or sister.

Everyone has done this at some time. There's a story about a man getting told off by his boss. He goes home and snaps at his wife

Feelings 7

because the meal isn't ready. She shouts at her son for not hanging up his coat. He teases his little sister till she cries; and she goes off and pulls the cat's tail. (No one knows what the cat does about it!) It's as if the bad feeling was a hot potato which burns our hands, so we quickly pass it on to someone else. And it's as if we all believed that we would not feel so bad ourselves once we had hurt someone else. What a strange idea! And yet, as I said, we all do it at times.

How bad feelings build up

If we can be like this over one single thing, think what it must be like to get hurt day after day: to be a Pakistani child in a district where Asian people are unpopular, or so disabled that people are embarrassed to be seen with you. Such people are often wonderfully patient and understanding about this; but why should they be? Being hurt can be the start of many problems.

When there's a story in the paper about an old man getting mugged, or a phone booth being vandalised, someone will probably make a comment about "yobs" or "mindless violence", as if there were no reason at all for it. But the reason may be that the mugger or vandal has been hurt through most of his life. If his mother was depressed and couldn't take much interest in him, if his father was often away, or beat him more than he hugged him, if his teachers made him feel that he was stupid or clumsy, if other children bullied him or laughed at him, if he left school feeling a failure, if no one would offer him a job, of course he will grow up feeling bad and worthless. His response may be, "If you make me feel bad, I'll be bad!" He now frightens people and at last he feels powerful. Of course what he does is wrong, but perhaps we can understand him.

It is as though bad feelings are like a poisonous or explosive liquid, and people are like the jars it is poured into. If a jar is strong it can hold the dangerous stuff – but don't put in too much or even that one will explode! A person who is always cross is like a container which is leaking; she or he is so full of bad feelings that there is no room for any more, and they trickle out all the time. And someone who is violent or has a

Feelings

quick temper is like a jar with a hole in it; any bad stuff which goes in spurts out straight away at someone else.

Things which hurt us may be small, middle-sized or big. When we are trying to deal with a big sadness, there is no room in our "container" for anything else, so we easily blow up at any little thing. And that can help, because when we let out our feelings about it, we get rid of some of the feelings about the big thing too. If we are lucky the people round us will understand this.

But I hope that the things which hurt you are small and only come once in a while. Most of us can contain small annoyances, unless there are too many all at once. The jar fills up and up, with no time to get rid of any of the bad stuff safely, and suddenly the next little thing is too much! We start shouting or crying, or doing something wrong. Everyone is amazed we got so upset over a trifle, because they didn't realise how much bad feeling we were already trying to hold inside. (You will notice the same reaction in a baby who is tired.) I once had a teacher who was fairly easy-going. But if we came into class and saw a tiny red flag drawn in a corner of the blackboard, we knew we had to behave extremely well. The flag meant, "I've already had all I can take today!"

Let's now find out if we can understand why Peter cut up the sweater. We can see part of it easily: he was full of excitement about his new baby and it all went wrong, and when he needed his mother to comfort him she was too ill and upset for herself. So he was full of very painful feelings. We shall have to guess at the other part. Perhaps it was something like this: "Why should Julie's mother give her a new sweater, when my new sister was stolen from me?" His feeling of pain turned into jealousy, and it seemed as if it would get better if he hurt someone else. I expect that still sounds strange, but think about it. I have sometimes felt like that. Have you?

Holding it in or letting it out?

So is it better for us to let out our feelings or to keep them inside? **There are two troubles with letting out your feelings – it is often unfair on someone else, and it doesn't really get rid of the weight you are carrying.** Peter may have felt better for a very short time, but before long he would feel the loss of the baby and his worry about his mum as badly as ever. On top of that he was now in trouble about the sweater. Even if he wasn't found out, he would still feel bad towards Julie. One thing I learnt from the older boys I worked with was that even people who have done lots of very bad things still feel guilty about what they do. A boy who had broken a window might say, "I was angry at Donald, but I didn't want to hit him!" I would be cross about the window, but I knew he had a conscience, because it stopped him hitting Donald.

You may say that as long as you take out your feelings on the person who caused them, that is all right, and you needn't feel guilty. There is some truth in this, it's certainly fairer than hurting an innocent person like Julie. But it doesn't always get rid of those upset feelings; you may still be thinking, "Was it true, that thing she called me?" And the other person is now feeling hurt by you, so you certainly haven't done anything to make peace between you!

As we saw, we may hold our feelings in because we're afraid someone will hurt us again if we show how angry and upset we are.

Feelings

And at home there can be another reason. We've been taught to be loving and kind to other members of the family. That's a good thing, but it may make it hard to admit it when we're not feeling loving towards them in the least!

But there are problems about holding the feelings tight inside you. It takes a lot of effort; sometimes so much that you can't think about other things or enjoy life. Have you noticed how, when you're trying to deal with upset feelings, you can't concentrate on your favourite TV programme? A worry which goes on for weeks will affect your schoolwork, your interests and your friendships. Indeed there are people whose whole lives have been spoilt because of something which happened to them when they were young. They are still holding it like a heavy secret inside them. A boy said to me once, "It's as if there was a great big eye inside me which is crying all the time." These experiences may have been big, or quite small. For example, there are grown-ups who are afraid to read aloud; and if you ask one of them about it, they may remember a time when the whole class laughed at them or a teacher punished them for reading badly. Others are afraid of the dark or have difficulty making friends. Such problems go back to childhood hurts and feelings which were held inside for too long.

We can find safe ways to contain these feelings so that they don't do harm to us. And we can find safe ways of letting them out which won't do harm to other people. Some people can find these ways on their own. But many need the help of a friend who can be a peacemaker for them,

helping them with their bad feelings and building bridges between them and those who hurt them.

That is what the rest of this book is about. In a world with so much conflict and unhappiness, we shall need as many peacemakers as possible. In fact we need everyone, including you, to grow up as a peacemaker. This isn't just to deal with wars, and unjust governments, and terrorists, and crime and violence. We need them wherever there is unhappiness in a neighbourhood, or a school, or a family, or in one lonely person.

Chapter Two:
CARING AND LISTENING

Imagine that two children whom you know have a fight or a quarrel, and one walks away upset. Perhaps you would like to run after him or her to help. What will happen if you do? Will he refuse to speak to you, but let you walk beside him? Will she angrily tell you to get lost? Will he start to make excuses for himself and complain that the other boy is always getting at him and doesn't fight fair? Will she burst into tears when she realises you are being kind to her?

I suppose any of these things might happen. And if your friend refuses to speak, or tells you to "get lost!" you will know that it's not always easy to be a peace maker. But before deciding, "It's no use trying to be kind to this one!" let's try to understand what's making them like this.

They are full of hurt and angry feelings, which they are trying to contain because they lost the fight or argument. You are the only person with them. So if they turn angrily on you, they are trying to pass their bad feelings on to you, like a potato too hot for them to hold. What can you do? You might feel like answering back, "Don't shout at me! I was only trying to help you. No wonder you don't have any friends!" If you do this, of course, you are simply handing back the hot potato (your own feeling of annoyance) and hurting them again, which is just the opposite of what you wanted to do.

Instead, try thinking of them as a container which is now full of a lot of bad stuff which they can't deal with – yet. So some of it spills over onto you. The way you can contain it is by not answering them back. You weren't part of the quarrel, so it should be easier for you to contain some of those feelings for them until they are ready to deal with them. Often this will happen very quickly. I remember once stopping a fight, and the boy who was getting the worst of it began shouting and swearing at me. I didn't get annoyed because he was showing he trusted me to hold those bad feelings and not to hurt him any further. I can't recall if I said or did anything – perhaps I put my arm round him, and a moment later he was crying and sobbing, and showing how hurt he really felt. The anger was only like the froth on top, and underneath was the pain.

Being there

If they stay quiet, it may be because they are trying not to pass on the hurt by saying something harsh to you. Or they may be trying to deal with their bad feelings for themselves. Sitting by them in silence is likely to make you feel no use at all. But you aren't really useless. If someone has to carry a very heavy load up a hill, you may not be able to take it away from them (for instance, Peter's baby sister had died, and no one could change that). But it is enormously helpful on that hill to have the company of a friend quietly walking beside you.

Think of the poisonous liquid and the container again. This time, imagine that you and your friend make a container together. Their part of it is under pressure; so your part must be as strong and peaceful as possible. Don't worry about yourself, but think only of them. Say a silent prayer for them if you find that it helps. Give them a hug, or hold their hand, if that

Caring and listening

is something you would naturally do. Don't be worried if they start to cry. That is often the quickest and safest way to let out some of the pain.

When they are ready to talk it is helpful to remember that your job is still to be a container. I mean that you can do much more by listening carefully to what they want to say than by talking yourself. Even if they are being very unfair or untruthful, it is not important at this moment to put them right (this doesn't mean you agree!) You may want to advise them what to do, or show them where they went wrong, or cheer them up. But none of these things helps them with what they have to do first, which is to find a safe way of letting out the bad feelings. There are many ways of doing this, as we shall see, and one of the best is to share them with a friend like you. But this means that they, not you, should be doing the talking.

Perhaps we could try to make some rules or rather guidelines for helping in this way:

- Be there with them.
- Listen a lot, talk very little.
- Don't blame them, even if they caused the trouble.
- Don't feel you have to support them alone; try to get other help if necessary.
- Don't pretend things are right when they are not.
- Don't give advice unless they ask you, and keep it short if you do.
- Don't feel you have to take sides for or against them in the quarrel (even if they try to make you say you are on their side).

When people are hurt they feel as if they had been damaged, they feel smaller, less loved and less lovable. Your interest in their problems, your sympathy and support, are the way in which you can tell them that they are important and valuable. By caring you say, "You are still loved."

Dealing with the feelings

Most of the teenage boys I used to work with had problems with their feelings. Some of them were holding them tight inside, which made them depressed and anxious. They complained of being bored with everything; but it was really that they had so much to cope with inside that they had no energy left for outside interests. Many of the others could not control their aggression; I mean they shouted at people, quarrelled, sulked, lost their tempers, smashed things, and easily became violent.

A group of them once sat together and wrote a little book called *Coping with your Temper*. It contained their suggestions to help one another, and they came up with twenty two ideas. I am going to share several of these with you. They may be useful when you are supporting a friend who is upset, but remember, don't give advice unless they ask for it. And, who knows, you may find one of the ideas useful for yourself at some time!

Go somewhere quiet. Get yourself right out of the situation that's making you upset – go and sit up a tree or lock yourself in the toilet!

Loud music. Listening to loud aggressive music like heavy metal can often help you to work out aggressive feelings. It's amazing how calm you feel afterwards.

Work it off. Sometimes you can get rid of your aggression by doing a hard job of work, like doing the dishes or digging – and you might earn a bit of money, which can't be bad!

Laughing and Crying. Intense feelings are very closely related -sometimes a fit of anger can suddenly turn into a fit of laughter or tears. If you can turn your anger into laughter, that's okay, and sometimes it helps you to see the funny side of things. There's nothing wrong with having a good cry – and often that's a better way of releasing your emotions than losing your temper.

Off-load your guilt. Sometimes you feel angry because you're feeling guilty about something. Tell someone what your guilty secret is, get it off your chest.

Caring and listening

Violent drawings. Jagged lines, explosions, bright colours – take your temper out on a piece of paper.

Swear! Go somewhere and shout – loud – at the top of your voice. But not at the person who is annoying you, or you might end up in a fight!

Write a note. If you really need to say something to somebody but you know you might lose your temper while you're doing it, write it all down in a letter, and get someone to take it to them. Some people write a first letter and tear it up, and are then ready to write a better one.

Physical exercise. Almost any form of physical exercise is good for working off tension. Go for a run or a long walk. Kick a ball against the wall. We sometimes hit a punchball with a face painted on it.

Do you have another suggestion to add to these, something which you have found helpful when you or your friends are upset? I've left a space for you to write it in:

Most of these ideas are to use in an emergency. But our group also had ideas to stop frustrated feelings from building up over a long time.

Keep a pet. It's nice to have someone or something to cuddle when you're feeling low.

Sleeping. It may sound pretty corny, but often when you're feeling tense or upset, a good night's sleep can put you right. Certainly if you're a person who is prone to be bad tempered, you should try to get regular sleep. If you're tired you're irritable.

Relax. It stands to reason that you can't be angry and relaxed at the same time. There are some methods you can learn to put yourself in a very relaxed state. They are easy to learn. (More about this in Chapter Six.)

If you can learn (and help other people) to manage sudden feelings and to let them out gradually and safely in some of these ways, you will not be in danger of harming other people or yourself. It's only after you learn to do this that you can really use

Caring and listening

your anger in the right way. It isn't wrong to be angry. It was Bob Geldof's anger at the pictures of dying African children on TV which saved so many lives. It was Dr. Barnardo's anger at the sight of children sleeping on roofs and in gutters that led him to open his first Home, with the sign, "No destitute child ever turned away." When Jesus drove the merchants out of the Temple, it was because he was angry at their greed and disrespect. We need people who can use their anger in the right way. Chapter Four will be about what can be done in situations which make us angry.

"What else could I do?"

When we have hit out, or shut ourselves away in sulks, we may say afterwards we didn't know what else we could do. This shows that we need to learn new ways to handle the situations which upset us. One thing which can be practised is the art of negotiation. **In negotiation you stick up for yourself (or someone else) and ask for what is**

right, and explain why, without getting angry or embarrassed or annoying the person you are talking to. If the two of you need a neutral person to help you sort it out, that is called mediation, and I'll say more about it in the next chapter.

The other thing to practise is thinking it over if you get upset. This is a mixture of things: **weighing up truthfully whether you might have done something wrong, trying to understand why the other person or people behaved in that way, and looking at your whole relationship with them.** How good is it? How would you like it to develop? Is it right to let this one thing spoil it? Can things be put right between you, and if so, how? You can see how much a thoughtful friend might help in thinking things over – or a group of friends as long as they don't talk too much but help you to work out your own conclusions.

The more you practise negotiation and thinking things over yourself, the less you will need that list of emergency measures, and the more you can be a peace maker for others.

But it won't be easy. At times you'll feel awkward and stupid. It can seem as if you are drowning in someone else's unhappiness, powerless to rescue them or yourself. You may never know if you were any real help to your friend. But what can be more important than trying?

Bryan was in a real temper one morning. He had been doing a cleaning job; and instead of someone putting his breakfast to keep hot it was left cooling in his place. And someone had nicked the piece of bacon. He demanded more, but there was no hot food left. He picked up the plate, threw it on the floor, and walked out through the mess. Albert, who got up without a word and went out after him, was a boy who had a very short temper himself. Our staff never knew what he said to Bryan or how he got round the cook. But a few minutes later he brought Bryan in smiling with a plate of toasted sandwiches, helped him to mop the floor, and sat down with him. Everything was peaceful again. Because Albert was starting to understand his own problems with his temper, he could help someone else.

Chapter Three:
BUILDING BRIDGES

One of the guidelines we had for listening to someone who is unhappy was "Don't feel you have to take sides for or against them in the quarrel (even if they try to make you say you are on their side)." You will find this is often difficult. Whatever upset them will also make them feel lonely. They may try to get rid of this feeling by trying to make you join them against their "enemies". What should you do? There will be times when you want to give someone who has been mistreated one hundred per cent support, as we shall see in the next chapter. But what if you actually disagree with what they have just done? If you tell them that they won't want to know you. So when you are trying to comfort someone, it is very tempting to agree with them that the other person is a beast and they were perfectly right, even though you don't believe it.

Don't take sides; don't blame people

You may ask, what's the harm in that if it makes them feel better? Well, firstly, you're now encouraging them in thoughts and behaviour which will lead to further hurt and disappointment. Secondly, they may not believe, deep down, that what they did was okay. Imagine someone holding your arm and screaming, "I was right, I was right, go on, say I was right!" Don't you think that they probably feel they may have been wrong? So if you pretend to agree, they will guess you are lying out of kindness. Then they can't trust the other things you may want to say. Do you see how this spoils your chances to help?

When people are angry and frightened, they don't see clearly what they – and those on the other side – are doing. I was a small boy during the 1939–45 war, and I remember how everything our forces did was described as brave and necessary, while everything the Germans did was evil, cowardly and underhand; and we all believed this was entirely true. Small boys in Germany of course believed exactly the opposite! Neither side had a true picture.

But a peace-maker must be able to see the rights and wrongs on both sides. This doesn't mean that you must start by pointing out where your friend went wrong. Remember that another of our guidelines was "Don't blame them, even if they have caused the trouble." Sometimes it's enough for you just to listen. Often they will go on for a time about how horrible the other person is, and then start talking about themselves. But if they want you to say who you think is to blame, it may be enough to say, "Tell me how you're feeling first," or "Look, I'm your friend – that's the main thing."

If you pretend to take your friends' side when they have been upset, will you be able to build bridges between them and those with whom they have fallen out? You can't build a bridge over a gulf if you are firmly on one side; you have to be able to move freely between the two sides.

Patterns of behaviour

In many cases you can't put all the blame on either side. Even in behaviour which is totally wrong, like bullying, the victim may keep doing something which brings the bully back. I remember when I was a teacher how a boy called Robert kept hitting a much smaller boy called Bill, who always ended up in tears. I wanted to punish Robert, but luckily I discussed it with the other children first. They told me that Bill kept annoying Robert till Robert attacked him. I asked why he did this, since he always got hurt. They said that Bill was so small that he did not dare hit anyone, but he used this way to get other boys into trouble. So the problem was not how to stop Robert; it was how to help Bill to change. We had to find out why Bill kept behaving in a way which meant he got hurt.

Family rows sometimes have a pattern like this. The child, for instance, keeps disobeying the mother; the mother doesn't deal with it

Building bridges

herself, but tells the father when he gets home; the father punishes the child, but then the mother says he is being too strict; the parents start having a row; the child, seeing they don't agree about how to deal with it, is disobedient again.

Who started it? That doesn't matter. The important thing is that a pattern of behaviour has developed; each person's action fits onto the next one almost like a jigsaw puzzle. If you watch these patterns you will see that when one person tries to break out of the pattern, the others pull her or him back into it. **The peacemaker has to look for ways to alter the pattern, and not take sides with any of the people in it.**

There are other sorts of pattern which you may notice. One is the feud or vendetta. There is a very good example in *Huckleberry Finn* by Mark Twain, where two families fight each other till in the end everyone is dead; yet no one can remember who committed the original wrong. Huck Finn, coming into the middle of it, at first takes one family's side but he comes to realise they are equally to blame. Another example comes in Shakespeare's *Romeo and Juliet*.

An arms race is something like this, but without the open violence. Two countries fear each other. Each time one gets the added protection of a new weapon, this frightens the other into increasing its own arms. Now the first one feels unsafe again and adds to what it has – and so on. This pattern is called escalation. It happens in smaller conflicts too. To the two opponents it seems the only way to remain safe. But the peacemaker can see that each step adds to the danger of war, like a snowball getting larger as it rolls down hill.

Peacemaker needed!

I want to look at the work of building bridges when you are trying to make peace between two people. It is also called mediation. Let's start by imagining some of the places where bridge-building is needed – and perhaps you can think of the sort of situations which might arise in each of them:

The Peace Kit

Building bridges

- A factory
- A back street in a city
- A school playground
- A sports field
- A youth club
- A police station
- A shop
- A family
- The frontier between two countries
- The lane between two housing estates ... and so on

In each of these situations you will probably hear anger on the surface: "They shouldn't be allowed to get away with it!" "They'd better not try anything on us!" There are other feelings, but they are often hidden. But after all we have thought about, you will realise that both sides feel hurt at whatever has already been said or done to them. There is fear that there will be more hurt to come. If there used to be a good relationship, there will be some sadness that it is spoilt. There is guilt, and I expect that this too will be found on both sides, because both have probably said or done things they aren't very proud about.

It sounds like a tough job for you or me to help make peace amid all these unpleasant feelings. But do you know the legend of Pandora's box? After she had opened it, and all those troubles had escaped and flown out into the world, one tiny creature followed them, and it was called Hope. There must be a true meaning in that story, because in these situations too there is a tiny hope. I don't mean our hope of improving things, I mean the hope of people caught up in the conflict that they can find a way out of it. How can we help both sides to work together for that hope?

Calming a situation

Let's think about a playground argument, because I'm sure you can easily picture one. Imagine that two children who were "best friends" yesterday are screaming at each other, while other girls and boys either egg them on or try to keep them apart.

Look first at the other children who are there. Some are taking no notice, either because they are too busy with their own interests or because they think the argument is silly. Some are enjoying it, laughing and cheering the two on or taking sides with one against the other. Some are bothered, and are frantically begging the two to calm down and leave each other alone. The grown-up supervisor has noticed what is going on and is just about to tell the two children off. The supervisor can probably calm the noise, but that won't build any bridge between the two of them. In fact nobody is bringing any peace into the situation, not even those who are trying to stop it.

What does a really peaceful group of people look like? Think of a group laughing together, telling stories, singing songs or playing a game. Think of them exchanging serious thoughts, or sharing in a job of work they want to get done. You see, "peaceful" doesn't mean quiet or boring. In that kind of a group it would be much easier for the two to forget their disagreement and join in with everyone else. They would find the satisfaction of sharing something good together.

How could you change the angry situation into the peaceful one? Sometimes it will be impossible; but I'm sure you have seen someone stop a row from blazing up by making a joke which got everyone laughing. I have known a boy interrupt a quarrel between two of his friends by starting a football kickabout. Everyone else began playing, and the two quarrellers decided to join in. The game helped them to let out some of their tense feelings without hurting anyone, and they walked together at the end as if nothing had gone wrong.

Being a go-between

But it is often not as easy as this. Let's now imagine that it is two or three days later, and your two friends have refused to speak to each other since the quarrel. You may find yourself going to and fro

Building bridges 27

between the two to make peace. This is how the government mediation service ACAS works to solve disputes between workers and employers. The two parties sit in different rooms, and all messages between them are carried by ACAS workers. There are guidelines for this work:

> Listen carefully to what each has to say. You may find they have quite different views about what started the argument and what it is about.
>
> Refuse to carry messages which are threats: "Tell him I'll kick his head in if he comes near me!" Ask them to say instead what it is they are angry about.
>
> Don't waste time discussing who's in the right. Use the time to help each one understand the other's feelings.
>
> Find out if this problem is like others which one or both of them had in the past. If it is part of a pattern, ask questions like, "Each time she does that, you do this. What would happen if you did the exact opposite?"
>
> You shouldn't pass on everything you are told – if you're not sure, say "May I tell him that?" But don't make things seem better than they are. It's very tempting to say things like "She's getting over it" to persuade the one you are with to be more friendly – but don't say anything that's not true! When they find out, they won't trust you any more.
>
> Find out what they each need and hope for in the future. Perhaps the quarrel arose when one disappointed the other, who now needs to feel he or she won't be let down again. If they can agree on what they both want, many of the differences will sort themselves out.
>
> If it is a very confused story, begin with the part which is simplest and easiest to sort out.
>
> You can feel very important and powerful when you are doing this work. Be careful not to get big-headed! Remember that the only agreement which will work is the one which they choose,

Building bridges

not the one which you think is best. You may do better if you and some friends work together as a group.

If you manage to build the bridge between them and they make friends again, don't be surprised or disappointed if they seem to lose interest in you. Perhaps one thing you did was to fill the gap for a time when they were missing each other's friendship.

At some point in the peace process the two will have to come together to sort it out. You can think of a quarrel as a conversation which got broken off half way through. Very important things were said, and people expressed their anger; but they haven't yet talked the thing through and settled it. Peace comes when the conversation is finished satisfactorily. This is the process called negotiation which I said was so important, and you can practice and develop your skill at it. I sometimes set this up in drama lessons – asking a young person to take back a faulty purchase to a grumpy shop assistant, for example.

Some people prefer to negotiate on their own after a disagreement. But if they want friends to be there as mediators, there are several things the friends should remember:

- Don't let them spend too much time trying to seem in the right or blaming each other.
- Each of them needs to hear and understand the other's hurt feelings.
- They should look at how they normally behave to each other, and decide if they want to change this.
- Each of them may have to promise to do (or not do) something for the sake of the other.
- Finally it will help to talk more about their hopes for the future than about the past.

There are many ways of solving problems between people, and some interesting games have been invented to practise these. If you think your class teacher, school teacher or youth leader might enjoy trying some of them with your group, you could suggest that they get a book called *Creative Conflict Resolution* by Bill Kreidler (details are at the back of this book). In some schools some pupils train as mediators to help the others; I have been involved in several of these schemes, and they do a very good job.

Peace-making in the family

Rows in the family are not so different from quarrels between friends. But bridge building can be more difficult, and it's much harder for me to give you any suggestions on how to do it. That's because each family has its own way of doing things. Children are allowed to say things in one family which they would never get away with in another! In one family there are great differences between how grown-ups and children can react to the same type of experience; in another, things are much more equal. I'm not going to say that one way is better than another, except that I'm sure violence never really helps.

A further complication is that each member of the family has her or his place in the family pattern. A row or upset in the family has its effect on everyone. I have suggested that the peacemaker shouldn't take sides; but in the family everyone is involved. Yet in spite of all this, we can help to build peace in our families.

You may be surprised if I say that the first rule is to allow conflict to happen! If everyone has to behave perfectly to everyone else in the family; if they are shocked if you get angry; if the children can never say they think something is unfair; if the grown-ups make all the decisions without discussing them with the children; if only the grown-ups or only the children are allowed to show what they feel: then family life will be very unpeaceful because it will be full of bottled-up bad feelings.

This doesn't mean that arguments are always a good thing. I remember times when our own children were teenagers, when we seemed to be having the same argument again and again. We had got stuck in a bad pattern. As we saw in Chapter Two, people who show their feelings aren't usually looking for arguments, but want to be

Building bridges

heard and understood. For some reason we failed to do that, so the rows went on.

It may be worth looking at the whole family pattern. Does everyone get a share of the good bits of family life? Or is it always the same person who does the work, and keeps in touch with absent members, and does the worrying for you all? If one person does nearly all the giving, and another only takes, there is conflict in the family even if it is hidden. The peace-maker may be able to take some of the load off the first person, or encourage the second one to give more. Because there is nearly always a peace-maker in the family. It may be granny, or one of the children. When I watch them at work I notice several things:

- They don't play the know-all, or say "I'm better than you."
- They are good at interrupting rows before they go too far, and turning them into peaceful situations.
- They sympathise with whoever is upset without blaming someone else.
- They are good "containers": they don't easily get upset themselves.

So what is a peaceful family? I think it should be like a good and loving little society where everyone is important. It has fairness and understanding; it doesn't expect any of its members to be perfect, and each of them can get help in dealing with their bad feelings. When someone gets into real trouble, he or she can count on the rest of the family to help put things right. The family won't be afraid of anger or other powerful feelings, because they know that we all feel strongly at times, and they know that the love in their family is still stronger.

Chapter Four:
MEETING FEAR AND PREJUDICE

Karen was small, timid and spoilt by her parents. At boarding school she was disliked and often left out of things. When Harriet started to go round with her, everyone said, "She only wants a share of Karen's parcels from home." Harriet was also unpopular, but this was because most of the children were a bit frightened of her. When she took Karen under her wing, the others did not dare tease the smaller girl any more. Harriet encouraged her to play netball; she was not very good, but everyone could see how hard she tried so as not to let her new friend down. Privately she told Harriet that she wanted to be admired and popular. Harriet could understand this because she too wanted to be liked better, and she helped Karen to get accepted.

It meant a lot to Karen to be chosen by this girl, whom everyone else held in awe; and by the time that their friendship faded out she could stand up for herself much better. Harriet afterwards admitted, "At first I joined up with her mainly for the sweets she was always getting. But you know, there was something else. I think it was good for me to look after someone else for a bit, and help her to get tougher. I really got to like her, you know – still do."

Some people aren't easy to like

Some people are unpopular through prejudice: that is, they are fat, or of a different race or a group which people dislike, but it is no fault of their own. But others are people whom it is hard to like, and if you try they may prove to be difficult friends. When our son Graham was thirteen he tried to be friends with a rather awkward and unhappy boy. Philip was glad to have a friend because he was unpopular, but he couldn't bear to share Graham with anyone else. He tried to force

Graham to choose between him and his other friends. It was rather like the situation we discussed at the start of the previous chapter. There was nothing for Graham to do but say, "These others are my friends. So are you. If you don't want it that way, that's for you to choose. But don't say it's my fault."

Yes, someone who is not liked is often not an easy friend. But you may find that like Karen she or he is nicer and more fun than the others think. There's another thing too. Unpopular people get a good deal of blame. But they don't really listen to it; instead they think, "People are only saying that because they don't like me." Once you have proved that you really do care for them they will listen to you when you suggest ways in which they might change themselves. This is because they know you're saying it out of friendship and not to tease or upset them.

When someone is mistreated

But there will be times when the problem is not just unpopularity but something worse. Cruel teasing and bullying makes me very angry. It is hard for me not to hate anyone I see doing it. But I know that if I attack them it does not stop them for long, and it makes me nearly as bad as them. **It is possible to hate injustice without hating the person who causes it.** So let's try to understand their problem.

Why are people cruel? Earlier we saw that it might be their way of trying to get rid of their own bad feelings, by hurting someone else. It might be because they had been hurt in the past, or because they were being bullied, or even (like Peter at the start of this book) because of problems at home. If this is the reason it will only make them worse if we hurt or hate them. We will be adding to the bad feelings which are already pouring out of their containers onto the overweight girl or black boy in the class. The boy who bullies (or girl, because girls can be very cruel too) needs help with his feelings of hurt and anger, but it is difficult to help because bullies surround themselves with an atmosphere of fear.

Meeting fear and prejudice

Fear cannot lead to peace. Indeed many would say it is fear which destroys the chances of peace. Fear and hurt are closely connected. If you think of the things which frighten people – snakes, the dark, falling, drunkards, hooligans, knives, guns, bombs, punishment, bullying – most fears come from thinking you will be hurt or remembering when you once were.

Why should bullies enjoy making the people round them afraid? Look at it this way: if people are scared of you, maybe you needn't be afraid of them. In other words, suppose bullies and hooligans are themselves secretly afraid, their frightening behaviour helps them feel a bit safer. You can imagine them thinking, "If people don't like me, at least I'll make them scared of me!" Is this why hooligans prefer to go round in gangs? Are they afraid to be on their own? Is this why bullies so often get their so-called friends to join in with them?

Can bullying be stopped?

If these guesses are right, we might be able to stop bullies by helping them to feel safer and more popular. But you may feel that you are not interested in whether the bullies have problems; what about the problems of the boys and girls who get laughed at and attacked? I think that in order to stop bullying, we need to think about both.

You may also feel that you are not brave enough to do anything about it. I wouldn't blame you, and I wouldn't want you to get yourself hurt trying to stop it. What we need is a safe way to change things.

Fear makes the victims feel separate and alone. So let's make a list of people who might be on the victim's side. This may give us some ideas for action.

> *Fellow sufferers.* It might be helpful to get all those who are suffering from the bully together. As we know, it helps to share unhappy feelings. Victims need someone to talk to, even if it isn't possible to change what's happening. In this case each girl or boy feels frightened and alone, but together they may feel strong: strong enough, perhaps, to go to the person who is

frightening them, and tell them it has to stop.

What would the bully do then? Possibly try to get one of this group alone and threaten them or hit them. So the group may have to stick together most of the time, even going home together, and make it clear to the bully that they all care about what happens to any one of them. This often works. Even if it doesn't completely stop the bullying, they will feel better because they are doing something about their problem. And they may decide together that they could get help from one of the following sets of people.

Other children. When we discussed bullying in our Quaker children's meeting, everyone agreed that the other children who are not getting bullied don't like to see it happening, but most of the time they feel too scared to interfere. Someone did suggest that the other children could threaten to beat up the bully if he or she did it again. But we realised that this is like saying, "It's okay to beat people up for a good reason," and we didn't feel that was right. Besides, it might start a problem of "snowballing" violence in the school.

In one school where there was too much bullying, a group of children and two teachers made a lot of badges which said, I'm against bullying. They started to wear them and encouraged all their friends to wear them too. As more and more of the children – and teachers – were

Meeting fear and prejudice 37

seen displaying this message, the bullies saw that a lot of people disapproved of them. They hadn't realised this before, and began to worry about what they were doing. When some of them asked for badges to wear, the problem was soon over.

But the bullies may feel even worse inside when they see so many people joining up against them. Most bullies need to have a group around them; but it's usually true that they don't have many real friends. This is where it helps to understand how they feel inside. If someone gives up bullying, that's when the real peacemaker will be quick to make friends with them. That's a good way to help them not to start again – I've seen it happen.

Teachers. Peacemakers quickly learn that they are not always successful. You will certainly come across unfair and unkind behaviour which you and your friends cannot stop on your own. There might be times too when everyone is so scared that you are not able to form a group to protect the victims. The bully has managed to separate them from everyone else. If you side with them, you too will be on your own.

Probably there are grown-ups who could stop it. But in most schools the children have a strong tradition against going to them, using words like "sneak", "grass" or "telltale-tit" to attack you if you do. The bullies are keen to enforce this; of course they are, because it is their protection. Would you dare to go to the teachers? Would you think it right? If you think you should, try to find at least one friend who is brave enough to go with you.

Here is something else which Graham did when he was thirteen. He had moved to a new school where there were a few Indian and Chinese children. Some bigger children were treating them very badly. Graham was new and he could have become very unpopular if he had started by telling tales to the teachers. But he did something a little different. He went to the ones who were to blame and said, "If you don't leave those kids alone, I shall go and tell the teachers about it." They knew he meant it, but they couldn't say he told tales on them. They stopped doing it; and although Graham was willing to become unpopular for what he thought was right, it didn't turn out like that.

It will help to check if your school has an anti-bullying policy (nearly every school does). Get hold of a copy and read it. It tells you what your school has promised to do about bullying, what your rights are and how to get them.

Parents. It often happens that a boy or girl is bullied at school for a long time without telling their parents. A boy in this situation explained to me that he was always afraid of making it worse. Your parents may handle it in a way which embarrasses you. They will almost certainly take it to the teachers and, as he said, "It can be quite painful telling the story again to someone you don't like or trust as much as your parents." If the teacher doesn't handle the situation well, it may even make the bullying worse. Another reason for not talking to parents is when you feel they have enough worries already, and you don't want to give them more.

And yet, if you can it's worth telling your parents if you get bullied – and encouraging other victims to do the same. They would surely want you to tell them. It might be easier to talk to them if you are taking up some of my other suggestions or an idea of your own. Then you can say to them, "We're trying to do something about it; but we may need your help if it doesn't work."

If you add up all the people we have listed who would like bullying to stop, it comes to a good number. **It isn't necessary for the bully's victims to feel alone. There are enough of us to make sure that school is a place without fear, as long as we're brave enough.**

Being afraid of teachers

A school without fear is a place where no one need be afraid of a teacher, unless they have done something wrong. I wonder if you have had a teacher who was not just strict, but sarcastic and unkind? I had

Meeting fear and prejudice

several, but I think there are not so many like that nowadays. Now I am grown-up I ask myself, "Were they like that because they were secretly afraid of us children?" It seems an odd thought; but there must be some reason why they are like that.

It would be good to tell such teachers that you can work much better for them if they encourage you instead of frightening you. But it's difficult to find a way to do it. Perhaps your parents could do it for you. Or perhaps you could write the teacher a letter on your own, or several of you together. It sounds risky, doesn't it? That's because it's very hard to know what the teacher will do. Might it make him or her worse? That depends on the teacher, but it also depends on what your letter says. Does it

- tell the teacher that you want to work hard and do well?
- mention things you like about his or her classes?
- explain clearly what frightens you and stops you working at your best?
- give the teacher the feeling that you're not blaming but trying to make things better for everyone?

If you want to think about the idea, it would be worth writing out a trial letter to show to your parents and ask their advice about sending it. They may have ideas for improving it. And if you do send it, they will be sure to check with you how your teacher took it.

Fear in the wider world

Fear is an important subject because it is responsible for much bigger problems too. It is a daily experience for people in the rougher parts of big cities, in places where terrorists operate, and in war zones. We saw how fear created the arms race. Yet if you look at the reasons why countries go to war, or terrorists do such terrible things, you will usually find that there was a time when they and their people were badly hurt. Because nobody cared enough to help them then, they now believe (wrongly in my view) that violence is the only way left to respond.

Some of our friends in Northern Ireland, where we used to live, were members of the violent organisations involved in the conflict there. By "friends" I don't just mean that we knew them and talked to them, but we visited each other's homes, chatted and played with the children. Some of our English friends were shocked at this. But it's like making friends with the bully. And it's like the love and care we gave the boys we used to work with, who (everyone said) were bad and worthless. We learnt that people don't change because others hate them. They may change when they know someone cares for them.

Prejudice

What about prejudice against whole classes of people, such as gypsies and black people? I think it comes from two things. One is that people are rather afraid of whatever is strange and unknown. In the Irish city where I lived there was a prejudice against the "travelling people" who have the same way of life as gypsies. Where we now live in England it is sometimes against Muslims and black people. My wife and I have Muslim, black and traveller friends, who have shown us plenty of kindness. We know that there is the same mixture of good and bad in these communities as in our own. Their ways are sometimes much better than ours; and the differences often make us laugh together. We think that the world is better for having different races, just like different flowers, fruit and animals. **If we can get people to understand and enjoy these differences, the first nail holding up prejudice is pulled out.**

Before I describe the second nail, let me tell you a story from South Africa. Some years ago a Swedish woman called Greta wanted to help the children of unemployed black people who didn't have enough to eat. She asked a white women's group if they would help her open a nursery school where black women could be paid to care for children, and a good meal would be served every day. "We will gladly raise money for your idea," replied the Chairwoman, "as long as our members are not being asked to help in the nursery." The white ladies did not want actual contact with others who were black.

For several months not one member of the women's group went near the nursery (which is a lovely happy place, I've seen it). Then one morning Greta phoned the Chairwoman: "Can you help me? I've just got the soup ready for the children, and now my car won't start! Could you drive it down for me?" The Chairwoman saw the nursery for the first time. She was impressed by the bright well-run place, and very moved by the welcome which the children and women gave her. Things changed. The members of the group began to visit regularly, and they prepared and served an enormous Christmas party for the children.

Why is prejudice hard to change?

People who have strong prejudices don't want to give them up. That is because prejudice is fixed in place with two nails. The first, as we have seen, is ignorance about people who are different. **The second nail which holds it up is the hidden pain and fear in the prejudiced person.** Remember how Peter's pain about his baby sister turned to jealousy of Julie, and how the bully's fear of being alone and unpopular turned into prejudice against those who had done him no harm.

You may have heard the word scapegoat. It refers to a person who gets blamed and punished by others for whatever is wrong. It isn't really the scapegoat's fault, it's like blaming the weather forecaster because she says it will rain tomorrow. **The person who is hurt and angry inside looks for a scapegoat – someone to blame, someone to hurt. Victims of course need protection; and the person who is prejudiced and aggressive needs to be helped in ways we have already thought about by others listening and caring, and helping the hurt feelings to come out in ways which don't harm other people.**

Chapter Five:
PUTTING THINGS RIGHT

Julie was holding the cut up pieces of her sweater and crying. "I'm glad Mr. Robinson caned Peter," she said, "He deserved it!" You can't blame her for feeling like this. Perhaps after she got over her disappointment she might think about Peter and the baby's death, and feel sorry for him too. But she was really hurt, and it's just as important to care about her hurt as Peter's.

All the same, did it do any good that Peter got beaten? As I have said before, when we are hurt we often believe we would feel better if the hurt gets passed on to another person. This is fair only if it goes back to the person who caused it. But even then we may feel no better. **And the hurt hasn't gone away; Peter now has an extra hurt to carry.** Unless he gets help from somebody, he may become the sort of person who goes on hurting others in secret ways, stealing from the cloakroom, tearing up other children's work, spreading unkind rumours, or causing other sorts of trouble. This is one of the reasons why caning is not allowed in schools any more.

Once he is caught, Peter has a new problem. Besides his grief for the baby and his guilt about the sweater, he is ashamed that the whole school knows what he has done. We all want people to think well of us and trust us. **So what is needed is a way of making peace which is fair to Julie and makes her feel better, and also gives Peter a way back into everyone's good books.** Since teachers are no longer allowed to use the cane, new ways must be found for dealing with these situations.

It was the head teacher who had to deal with it. So let's try to guess his reasons for caning Peter. I think there were three. I'll put them on the next page, so you can make your own guesses and see if you agree with me.

I'm sure he was concerned about Julie's unhappiness. He was probably worried about what her parents would think. And I think he may have felt, "If I don't deal with this strictly, other children will think they can get away with this kind of behaviour." In Peter's case this last reason isn't a very good one; girls and boys don't usually want to cut up each others' clothes even if they think they can get away with it. **But with some sorts of behaviour it is important to show what will happen to people who do it.** People need to know, for instance, that they could be in serious trouble if they drink and drive. Punishing people as a warning to others is called deterrence. But would it be fair to punish wrongdoers more heavily than they deserve, simply to frighten the rest of us? For instance, to discourage thieves, you could be hanged in Britain two hundred years ago just for stealing a few books.

Being worried about what Julie's parents might think may not seem to you a very good reason either. But parents rightly expect teachers to make sure that children and their property are safe at school; just as we expect the police and law courts to keep us safe in society. I agree with Clare in blaming Mr. Robinson for what he did to Peter, but I realise that he has to keep order in his school. **What we have to ask is, what is the best way to do that?**

Advice for Mr. Robinson

Just pretend that you have the chance to advise Mr. Robinson. Before you read on, decide what you would say to him. Do you think your idea will satisfy everyone involved, Julie, her parents, Peter, his parents, and Mr. Robinson's need to keep order?

Remember that one of our guidelines for mediation was *Find out what they each need and hope for in future.* Julie wants a new sweater as nice as the one she lost; she also wants to feel sure Peter won't do it again. Peter knows what everyone is thinking about him; he needs a way to show that he is sorry about what he did, and can be good. Mr. Robinson has to be fair to Julie; he has to satisfy her parents that he did something effective; and he also has to help Peter not to behave like this again but ask for help when he is upset.

Putting things right

Is that everything which needs to happen, or have I overlooked something?

In my work with older boys we often had this kind of situation. We didn't leave it to grown-ups to make the decision. The whole school met and discussed it together. (This was possible because we only had forty five pupils.) What usually happened was that the boy in charge of the meeting asked the boy who had done wrong, "Are you willing to do something to put this right?" Nearly always the answer was "Yes". So he was asked, "What are you willing to do?" If he couldn't suggest anything, the other boys would make suggestions. When it was a broken window the answer would usually be, "He should measure the size, go to the village, buy a piece of glass, and mend the window." If he didn't know how to use putty an older boy would help him. In a case of bullying, he might say, "I'll work in the garden and earn enough money for Tom to go to the cinema on Saturday" (he might even offer to go with him!) If it was damage to something like a sweater, and it couldn't be mended, he would have to earn enough money to buy a new one as well as something else to make up for the hurt he caused. The boy was not forced to do some particular thing. He was asked to agree to something, and once he agreed, he nearly always did it. And because the other boys had shared in the decision they would encourage him, or complain if he didn't get on with it.

Showing that you are sorry

There are several things to notice about this. **The first is that it puts things right.** It's only fair that if someone destroys your property it should be replaced. If someone has made you cry, they should do something to make you happy. Justice is a very important part of peace-making.

Secondly, the offender hasn't got away with it. Several hours' work in the garden is no joke! But the difference between this and a caning is that, instead of being hurt in revenge, he has done something useful. And everyone has agreed the decision was fair.

It also helps to mend the relationship between victim and offender. If you are feeling sore at someone for what they have done to you, it makes a lot of difference if they then do something nice for you. Have you noticed what a fuss grown-ups make about you saying "Sorry"? Even if you don't mean it, they still feel better once you have said it. They will feel even better if you do something for them to show how sorry you are. But it should be done willingly; being made to pay for something out of your pocket money isn't the same as wanting to replace it. But I think that deep down people want to put things right when they have upset someone. Sometimes our boys felt so bad that they pretended they didn't care; but if a peacemaking friend took them off quietly to start putting things right, they were glad to have the chance.

And the last advantage is that it will change the way that the other people feel about the one who has done wrong. He or she is sending them a message: "Yes, you've seen that I can be bad,

Putting things right

but now you've seen that I care about what I did and I can be good too."

Do these ideas make sense to you? People sometimes seem to think that you could only be fair to Julie by hurting Peter; and you could only help Peter at the cost of being unfair to Julie. If you think in terms of punishment in this way, one of the two people won't get what they really need. **But the idea of putting things right is fair and helpful to everyone.**

Julie and Peter

Of course things can't always be put perfectly right. If the sweater had been knitted by Julie's granny before she died, no sweater bought in a shop could make up for it. Sometimes what is done to put things right is a second best, and we just hope that it will be enough to help with the hurt feelings.

In Peter's case, there is another problem. If he had been fifteen, he could have really worked to earn the full value of the sweater. If he had been five, he could have been asked to do a very nice picture for Julie, and write Sorry on it, and help his mother with some job everyday, and he would feel he had shown he was a good boy now. But Peter was too young to earn the full cost of the sweater, but old enough to understand what it would cost. His parents, not he, would have to pay for a new one. If they do so, how can Peter feel he has put things right? My family discussed this at tea the other day, and here are some of our suggestions:

> He might do something to help at home every day; in this way he would feel he was making it up to his parents for what they had to spend, and also helping his mother get better.

> He might be paid for some work by his parents, or someone else, even the head teacher – so that when Julie gets her new sweater he is able to tell her he earned five pounds of it himself to show he is sorry.

> He and his parents might invite Julie to come to town with them to choose a new sweater, and he might earn enough money to

buy her a present at the same time or give her tea in a cafe.

He might tell Julie he is sorry, and ask her to tea at his house, and do his bit by making cakes or sandwiches or whatever he could manage.

What else do you think he could do?

Guilty secrets

If I had known some of these ideas for putting things right when I was small, I might not have had guilty secrets from time to time. My parents weren't at all strict, but I found it very hard to own up to things I felt bad about. It would have been easier for me if I had thought of painting a picture or buying a bar of chocolate for them and saying, "I brought you this to say sorry, because I did something wrong."

Even if you think you can never say it, you still may feel better if you can do something – tidy the shed, or do the dishes, or cook some sweets. And if your mother notices that you have been extra helpful and says so, that might be the moment when you find you can say, "Well, I'm doing it because I feel bad about something..."

Forgiveness

Putting things right, challenging injustice, building bridges, and listening and caring are ways of helping someone who is hurt to get ready to forgive the person who did the hurting. Sometimes all four are needed, sometimes one or another is less important. But many people will say, "Why should they forgive? They've been hurt, haven't they? They have a right to their anger!"

Perhaps we don't always have a right to our anger. When people remain angry this is sometimes because they don't want to admit that they should take a share of the blame. Susan makes a spiteful remark about another girl, who loses her temper and pulls Susan's hair. While

Putting things right

Susan is making a big fuss about this, she's not likely to admit that she hurt the other girl first by what she said. But very often we have every right to our anger, and that means we don't have to forgive. No one can make us. Indeed some things which people do are so horrible that it's hard to see how they could ever be forgiven.

All the same, the hurt only ends when it is forgiven. Do you remember the story when the boss told off the worker, who snapped at his wife, who shouted at her son, who teased his sister, who pulled the cat's tail? The hurt ran on and on. But if any one of them had forgiven the one who hurt him or her, it would have stopped. Just imagine a world where there was no forgiveness. All families, even the best of them, would be split by anger. Friendships wouldn't last long. People wouldn't trust each other. Workplaces would be full of angry, suspicious people. How would strikes end, and what feelings would be left behind when they were over? How would countries which had been at war ever make friends again, as the countries which fought each other from 1939 to 1945 have done? **Kenneth Kaunda, the President of Zambia said, "Unless we are able to forgive the enemies who cannot possibly make up to us for what they have done, we go stark raving mad with bitterness and hatred."** And you can see that people are forgiving one another in big and small ways all the time.

Are there things we can't forgive?

Some actions are so terrible that it seems impossible to forgive them. But I have seen people forgive even these. I know a man who did some of the killing in Northern Ireland. Later he was very sorry about what he did; he felt terrible and thought he could never be forgiven. And I know a woman whose husband was killed by the group to which this man belonged. There wasn't even a reason, he was killed in mistake for someone else. This man didn't know her or her story, and when they met he explained to her his terrible feelings of guilt. Then she told him how her husband died, and for a moment he thought he might have done it. Can you imagine how he felt? He asked the date and place, and said with relief, "Thank God it wasn't me!" She looked at him and said, "Tom, I wish it had been you, because then I could have shown you that I do truly forgive you." I can't be sure whether I could be so forgiving. I know I would like to be so. Two of the Northern Irish children who have already read this book have fathers who were killed by a terrorist group; and both of them said that what I have written about forgiveness is right.

You may think it is better to accept that something has happened and to decide, "Nothing can be done about this, I'll just try to forget it." Sometimes this is the best that can be done. But it is a way of giving up; and I don't believe that anyone can give up and accept wrongs in this way, time and again, without becoming bitter. It doesn't help the other person either, who may be feeling very bad and looking for a way to mend their relationship with you. What is different about forgiveness is that it is a new start. It looks towards the future with hope for both of you. What was wrong is not just pushed away to one side. Instead you both learn from it to do better in future.

Christian forgiveness

I believe that what I have been saying in this book is true for everyone. It is the same whether you believe in God or not, and whatever church or faith you belong to. But I have to say too that my belief in the importance of forgiveness comes not only from what I have seen, but also from my Christian faith. Jesus believed very strongly in forgiveness and the steps towards it. I am not going to show you this in detail, but I will tell you where to look for it in the gospels. He spoke about the trouble that comes from bad feelings held in the heart (Mark chapter 7: verses 20–23). One of his most famous stories is about caring for the hurt (Luke 10: 30–37), and there are many times when he listened to people in difficulties. He taught about building bridges (Matthew 5: 23–26). He was delighted when a dishonest tax-collector offered to put things right with the people he had cheated (Luke 19: 1–9). On forgiveness itself there is the story of the prodigal son in Luke 15: 11–32. He told his followers to forgive "seventy times seven" (Matthew, 18: 21–22). And he told us we would

Putting things right 51

be forgiven if we forgave other people. I don't think this was meant as a threat. Sydney Carter the songwriter (I expect you know "Lord of the Dance") once wrote, "Your sins are forgiven ... as soon as you see what is really happening. When you do, you will forgive others. If you can't ... you haven't really seen the way things are."

Chapter Six:
BECOMING A PEACEFUL PERSON

In the United States in the 1950s and 1960s, there were laws which took away many of the rights of black people; and they were badly treated by many state officials and by white terrorist groups such as the Ku Klux Klan. The black leader, Martin Luther King, once said to those whites: "Do to us what you will and we will still love you. We cannot obey your unjust laws ... so throw us in jail and we will still love you. Bomb our homes and threaten our children and, difficult as it is, we will still love you. Send your hooded perpetrators of violence into our communities at the midnight hour and drag us out on some wayside road and leave us half dead as you beat us, and we will still love you... But be assured that we'll wear you down by our capacity to suffer, and one day we will win our freedom. We will not only win freedom for ourselves; we will so appeal to your heart and conscience that we will win you in the process, and our victory will be a double victory."

What a strong container he must have been, and the black people who stood with him, to take all that hate and violence, and go on loving those who hurt them! This book has been about you helping to contain people's anger and unhappiness in quite small events, and you will find that even that can be difficult and tiring. How can we become strong enough to be peaceful in our everyday lives, let alone in such difficult times as Martin Luther King's?

Refusing to get into a fight

Have you ever felt that you had no choice but to get into a fight (a fist-fight or a quarrel) when you didn't want it? It may have been a brother or sister who wouldn't stop annoying you, or a grown-up who wouldn't listen to what you had to say – or other children who would

Becoming a peaceful person 53

call you "chicken" if you walked away. You may have felt that your container just wasn't strong enough to hold the anger you felt. Is there anything you could have done before it exploded?

My answer is: Yes, there may be, if you decide in time, before you say or do something which might hurt somebody or get you hurt. Try to contain your feelings just long enough to check four things:

- **Have I let them know what I feel about what they are doing?** (Sometimes people don't actually realise how annoying they are being.)

- **Am I being fair, or am I passing on a hurt which came to me from someone else?**

- **Is this person hurting me because they can't contain their hurt feelings about something else?**

- **Which is more important, the anger I am feeling or my friendship with this person?**

But the most important thing is to remember that you always have a choice what to do. Sometimes the choice doesn't look good either way, for example, getting into a fight or being called "chicken". But you may know that this fight is bound to lead to more problems; while if you walk away you may respect yourself more, and perhaps other people too will respect you. Or you may think it likely that this disagreement will escalate into serious trouble unless one of you is wise enough to back off. So it is worth weighing up the choices before you get to the point where you lose your temper Even people with quick tempers have some warning feelings (usually in their tummies) before they lose control.

There are times when most of us just can't cope. And that is why we need to train ourselves to be more peaceful people, stronger containers. This may sound impossible. But in fact there are simple ways of doing so, which you can practise every day.

Learn to relax

The first thing to practise is learning to relax. Do this every day until you find it is easy to get completely relaxed. You could do it twice, once in the day lying on the floor, and once when you go to bed and put the light out.

- Stand up with your legs apart and stretch up as high as you can. Try to reach the ceiling! As you stretch, take a long deep breath and hold it in.

- Let yourself flop forwards so that your fingers touch or nearly touch the floor and your head dangles down like a rag doll's. As your chest falls forward let all the breath come rushing out.
- Make yourself as limp as you can.

- Stretch and flop two more times

- Gently lie down on your back, with your arms on the floor by your side and your legs slightly apart. Keep your head facing upwards. Breathe in and tighten up all your muscles – your arms, legs, tummy, back and neck; even screw up your face!

Becoming a peaceful person

Then let everything go loose again, and at the same time let your breath rush out as if you were a punctured tyre. You should check if face or neck, fingers or toes are still tight. Make certain every bit of you relaxes. If you're not sure, tighten up once more and then relax again.

- Now feel your breathing going in and out. Try to feel it at the tip of your nose. It's cold going in and warm coming out. As you breathe out, feel how heavy your body is, pressing down on the ground; as you breathe in, feel your body becoming light, as if it could just float away. If other thoughts come into your mind, just blow them away as you breathe out and let them go. Allow yourself to become nice and drowsy.

- Unless you're ready to go to sleep, have a big stretch and a long yawn when you're ready to finish. Do this several times if you like. Then look around, and slowly sit up, wait a moment and then stand up. If you get up too fast you will feel dizzy and uncomfortable; so don't jump up, even if someone unexpected comes into the room.

If you have to sit down and wait for a few minutes during the day, practise the slow breathing. You can even do it when walking along, breathing in for four steps, holding it for two, and letting it out for four. If you come into a situation which makes you furious or panicky (even the dentist!) you will find you can use this deep slow controlled breathing to calm yourself. It works very fast!

A secret place of peace

When you are used to relaxing, you can practise something new as you lie on the floor. I want you to imagine a secret place which nobody can find but you. It may be that you have to go in through dark caves and passages, or crawl along rabbit paths under the thorns of the forest undergrowth. Or there may be a hidden door, and a winding staircase with wrong turnings which anyone except you would take. It may even need a boat or a rocket ship to get there. I don't know what your secret place is like, but it will need to be very peaceful for times when troubles come. Mine might be a hidden clearing in the forest with a grass floor and wild strawberries and the sun shining down through young leaves; or perhaps a small sandy beach which can only be reached through long tunnels in the rock. Yours might be an indoor room with a blazing fire, or a garden on top of a tower.

Relax first, and then imagine the tricky journey, passing the places where others would go wrong, till you come out at last in your peaceful place. As you lie there, enjoy the warmth, the flowers, or whatever it is that makes the place special for you. Don't think too hard about it, just picture being there. And when you think it is time to leave, say goodbye to it and imagine coming back along the secret ways into your everyday life. Always imagine the journey, going and coming back.

Take this journey in your mind when you relax, whenever you have time. It doesn't always have to be the same place, if you would like several to choose from. Your peaceful place is somewhere to go when your container is full of anger or worry or sadness. You may like to think of a friend who lives in your secret place who gives you help and comfort; it might be Jesus or some other wise and holy person, or someone you love who has died. You don't go there to talk over your worries with them, but to enjoy the peace of their company. But you will sometimes find that, after doing this, you know what to do next about a problem. Because this is a way to visit the store of peace which you have inside yourself, so that you can bring back peace for others.

When you do this regularly, you will find that it does make you a more peaceful person; and that will certainly help you to be a better peace-maker. And you can use your peaceful place in

Becoming a peaceful person 57

another way. When you are helping someone else who is upset and you don't know what to do, relax and imagine you are guiding them to it through the dark and difficult passages. When you both arrive you can lie on the soft sand, or grass, or fluffy carpet and enjoy the warmth and peace, not even talking about the problems they face. Or you can imagine introducing them to your wise friend and leaving the two of them talking while you explore or rest. Then think that you are bringing them back to real world and its difficulties. Even though your friend never knows you are doing this, you will be surprised to find it makes it easier for you to support them.

Peacemaking in the wider world

You might have seen a poster which says "Peace will come through ordinary people like you". And perhaps you felt that it was impossible that someone like you, on your own, could bring peace. If so, you were thinking about the ending of war. I hope I have helped you see that there is a lot every one of us can do to bring peace in a different kind of way, small compared to wars, but still very important. It's not much good waiting and hoping that one day your chance will come to stop a war! There's lots of peace waiting to be made near you every day.

And if you get on with that, you are getting yourself ready to deal with the big chance if it ever comes your way. I'm thinking about an eighty year old lady called Lucy Behenna, who was living in an old people's home in 1980, when people still thought that war between the Soviet Union and Western countries was very likely. She was rather old to start working for peace, you might think. But one day she saw that same poster. "It can't mean me," she said. And then she thought about mothers: "What's more ordinary than being a mother? And surely they don't want to see their children killed in a war!" And she had the idea of sending some British mothers to Russia (where few British visitors went at that time) and some to the USA, to talk to other mothers about this. First she and a friend put all their life savings into the idea, and then she travelled hundreds of miles asking other people to give what they could. Ten mothers made the journeys; other mothers came on a return visit to Britain from the USA and

Becoming a peaceful person

Soviet Union. They found that they all longed for peace. Lucy is dead now, but Mothers for Peace went on for many years, building hundreds of friendships between people who were once called "enemies".

You too can do something for peace. Start by choosing what kind of problem you will tackle and what change you would like to bring. It may be about the prejudices which cause conflict, or weapons of war, or unfair world trade which hurts and exploits poor people, or global warming which will damage the earth and set people fighting for resources which will become scarce (like water). Then you need to look for information – otherwise you are like someone shooting an arrow who can't see the target clearly. People say that knowledge is power, and you will find that the more you really understand a problem, the more power you have to address it. The internet has made this task very much easier for us.

For example, if you want to buy a certain make of T-shirt, you can go to the brand's website to see which country their shirts are made in, and what they say they do to help their local employees there. If there is no information the website will give you a contact link so that you can write and ask your questions. You can check their answers with an independent website like the Clean Clothes Campaign. If you decide that you don't want to buy those clothes because they are made by children in India, you can write to the company and tell them why you made this decision. When enough people protested to one company which employed children, they agreed to set up a school for the children in the factory, and let them work half the day and study the other half (the children liked this because they could go on earning money to help their very poor families and also get education which is the key to a much better job later).

Once you begin to understand a problem you can use your knowledge in many ways:

- ask the right questions in lessons such as geography and economics so that the other pupils and teacher also begin to understand the problem – this could lead to the class inviting a speaker from an agency like Oxfam

- write a letter to your local paper explaining the problem – or to your MP asking if he or she is aware of it and trying to improve things

- get a pen-friend in a country where there are problems and ask about his or her life (I work in Africa and the former communist countries, and I keep meeting teenagers who are learning English and longing for pen-friends) – or get to know local people who come from the part of the world affected to learn more about the issues and what needs to be done

- if you're lucky enough to go away on holiday to a developing country, check one of the websites I've listed on page 63 to find out how your family visit can help the people there instead of harming them

- join a local organisation which is working on the problem and offer them a bit of your time

- find out how to buy what you and your family need in ways which do not harm far-away workers or damage the environment

- raise some money to help people who live in the place where the problem is happening and are trying to change things (in our Quaker meeting the children used to organise a sale once a year to help overseas projects)

Don't ever feel that you are too unimportant to do something. Just before the 2003 war against Iraq, my grandson Jake wrote to the Prime Minister to say how afraid he was about the war. Because he was a child, in a few days he got a personal letter from 10 Downing Street answering his points. I wrote about the same time and had to wait for five weeks for a very generalised answer. Archbishop Desmond Tutu, one of the leaders in the struggle against injustice in South Africa once said, "If you think you're too small to make a difference, try spending the night with a mosquito!"

If one of these thoughts gives you an idea, try to follow it up. At least you will begin to understand more about other people and places.

Becoming a peaceful person

And the more you understand, the better chance there is that you will suddenly discover something to do which no one has thought of before.

* * *

Now that you have read this book, will it just lie on a shelf and get forgotten? Or are you going to put it into practice? If you want to do that, I can suggest two ways of using the book. One is to read it again, but only one chapter a week, say on Sunday. Then during the week, look out for ways of trying out the ideas in the section. The other is to keep it handy (so you don't forget about it) and whenever you are mixed up in an unpeaceful situation, look up what the book says about it, using the index of problems. See whether it gives any advice which you can use. Good luck with it! And don't forget to practise how to relax!

This page is for you to write down your own ideas

Acknowledgements, and Discovering More

I would like to thank Joanne Craig, Garrett Mallon, Paula-Marie Mullan, Edward McCay, Morgan Fullam, Zoe Alien, Alan Koenig, Alison Shaw, Nigel Reid, Kerry Orr, Brian Magill, David Mathers, Christopher Downey, Michael Cheung, Richard Watson, Shane Mathers, Ian Mathers, Jonathan Heaney, David-John Hunter, and their class teacher Elaine Marshall, who all gave so much help; the children of Bishop Street and Coleraine Quaker Meetings in Northern Ireland; and also Dalton Taylor, Mary and Don Gregory, and my own children Clare, Judy, Graham and Frank, who showed me how children can be peace-makers.

I owe special thanks to Cormac Downey who drew the pictures. Cormac was fourteen when he did them. This is the second book he has illustrated.

I am very grateful to my wife Diana, who is a yoga teacher, for help with the relaxation sequence; to a group or boys some years ago at Shotton Hall School and their house-father John McCardle, who wrote the booklet *Coping with Your Temper*; to the Ulster Quaker Peace Education Project for good learning experiences together; and to the Joseph Rowntree Charitable Trust who gave me time to write it.

Creative Conflict Resolution by Bill Kreidler is published by Good Year Books in America. A good general book on solving conflicts is ***Everyone Can Win*** by Helena Cornelius and Shoshana Fayre from Simon & Schuster in Australia. Both of these can be ordered from the Quaker Bookshop, 173 Euston Road, London NW1 2BJ.

Useful websites (see page 60) include: **www.responsibletravel.com** and **www.tourismconcern.org.uk** for checking out holiday destinations and **www.getethical.com**, **www.ethicalconsumer.org** and **www.cleanclothes.org** for thinking about what you buy. You might also look at **www.g-nation.co.uk** which shows young people how they can change the world by giving. There are thousands of sites which help you to understand better the world's problems which lead to war.

Quotations are from Coretta Scott King: *The Words of Martin Luther King* (Fount); Kenneth Kaunda and Colin Morris: *Kaunda on Violence* (Collins); and Sydney Carter: *The Rock of Doubt* (Mowbrays). Lucy Behenna's story is told in *Mother for Peace* by Sheila Ward (Quaker Home Service).

Index

Anger, 8-9, 14-20, 43-47, 48-51
Arguments, 5, 13-14, 5-32
Arms race, 21

Breaking things, 10, 15, 19, 45
Bridgebuilding, *chapter 3*
Bullying, *chapter 4*

Carrying messages, 26-29
"Chicken", 53
Christian forgiveness, 50
Containing feelings, 8, 13-17, 52, 56

Escalation, 22, 54

Family conflict, 11, 23, 30-32,
Fear, 10, 33-40, 56
Feelings, *chapter 1*, *chapter 2*, 26-29, 34-35, 47-49, 53
Feuds, 23
Fights, 13, 14, 23, 45, 52-54
Forgiveness, 48-51
Friends, *chapter 2*, *chapter 3*, 33-35, 37

Gangs, 35
Go-between, 26-30
Guilt, 10, 16, 25, 43, 48, 50

Holding feelings in, 8, 13-17, 53, 55-56

International peace, 49, 58-61

Jesus, 19, 50, 56

King, Martin Luther 52

Listening, *chapter 2*

Mediation, 23, 26-30
Minorities, 8, 32, 38-39, 48
"Mothers for Peace", 58-59

Name-calling, 6
Negotiation, 19, 23-26
Parents, 30-32, 38, 40, 47
Peaceful groups, 26, 59
Place of peace, 56-58
Prejudice, 8, 34, 41-42
Punishment, 5-6, *chapter 5*,
Putting things right, *chapter 5*

Quarrels, 5, 13, 26-32

Relaxing, 18, 54
Revenge, 6, 10, 36-37, 44, 49

Sadness, 8, 10, 14-15, 23-26
Saying sorry, 43-48
Scapegoats, 42
Secrets, 43, 48
Standing up for others, 33-34, 35-38
Standing up for yourself, 19, 33-34, 52-54

Taking it out on someone, 8, 10, 13, 52-53
Taking sides, 15, 21-25, 34, 36
Teachers, 5-6, 35-39, 43-44
Teasing, 34
Telling tales, 35-38
Temper, 8, 15-19, 48-49, 50-51
Terrorism, 37-38, 49, 52
Thinking it over, 19, 52-54

Unfairness, 14, 31, *chapter 4*
Unpopularity, 34-35, 38

Victims, 21, *chapter 4*, 49-51
Violence, 5-8, 15-16, 21, 22, 23, 33, 37-38, 45-47, 48-50

Work, 15, 42-46